Freedom from Psychological Prison:

How to break free from the shackles of emotional bondage

By

Marian D. Blake

TABLE OF CONTENTS

Introduction

Do you feel worthless, isolated, manipulated, scared or caged? Is your confidence and self-esteem low? Or perhaps there is someone around you who makes you feel like you are not good enough? These are a few of the many signs of emotional abuse. This book tells you what you need to know about emotional abuse and how to break free from its bondage because you deserve to be happy.

Overtime I have come across victims of emotional abuse and many do not realize they are living in bondage because of the nature of the abuse. Psychological maltreatment can manifest in several ways. It can occasionally ambush you and conceal itself in charming phases. Sometimes it comes in waves or total stillness. It can be challenging to recognize the signs of emotional abuse. Some of the indications might not be noticeable to you. Perhaps you have been misled into thinking that all relationships are like this or that you are very sensitive. However, you may want to take more notice if you begin to feel alone, helpless, or unworthy in your relationships.

You have no valid cause to feel this way. You deserve kindness, affection, and respect.

It is also important to know that anyone can experience emotional abuse at any point in life.

Emotional abuse affects adults, teenagers, and children alike. The effects of emotional abuse on relationships and all parties involved can be disastrous. The absence of a visible mark does not negate the reality of the abuse, its problem status, or the fact that it is illegal.

Researchers refer to emotional abuse as "chronic verbal aggression" or psychological assault. Individuals who experience emotional abuse frequently exhibit extremely poor self-esteem, personality abnormalities including withdrawing, and in extreme cases, suicidal thoughts, anxiety, or depression.

Similar to other forms of abuse, emotional abuse frequently manifests as a cycle. This cycle begins in a relationship when one party emotionally mistreats the other, usually as a way to assert dominance. The abuser subsequently experiences guilt, but more from the results of his or her actions than from what they have done. He or she then invents justifications for his own actions in order to escape accepting accountability for what happened then acts in a "normal" manner as though the abuse had never occurred.

In fact, the abuser may even be particularly endearing, generous, and regretful to give the abused party the impression that they are sorry.

The abuser also starts to visualize about manhandling his partner formerly more and creates an atmosphere where more emotional abuse can happen.

As you go through this book, you will observe that an emotional abuser can be a male, female, co-worker, boss, or family member. This is because it is not limited to gender, romantic relationships or status. It does not matter if you are rich, poor, educated and a worker, emotional abuse can happen to anyone.

If you are lost and do not know if you are psychologically abused or you realize it but have no idea of breaking free, this book will make you understand that despite the fact that we do not have total control of how people treat us, we can identify when we are emotionally abused, what to expect from an abuser and that we do not deserve to be treated in such manner and if you are already a victim, this book will guide you on how to break free, breathe again and never fall victim a second time.

Chapter 1
Psychological Prison: What it entails

It is commonly known as Emotional Abuse. Some people believe it is a sub of emotional abuse but for the purpose of this book, it will be regarded as closely related. Before we dive into emotional abuse, let us understand what the term "abuse" is.

Abuse is any action taken with the goal to exploit another person or cause them harm. When anything is done purposely to damage another person, it is considered abuse. Physically violent behaviors, sexual assault, neglect, and degrading treatment are all examples of this. A single instance of abuse may occur, or it may take the form of a pattern of behavior that appears again throughout time and in many contexts. Whenever abuse occurs, it is planned. It is possible to physically or verbally harm someone else without it being considered abuse. Abuse is not necessarily determined by the impact, but rather by the intention. In other words, someone might push you around and say cruel things to you with an aim of hurting you. Their actions count as abuse even if you are not harmed by them. This brings us to Emotional Abuse.

Its goal is to terrorize, dominate, or isolate the victim. Emotional violence can have just as negative of an impact as physical abuse. However, your wounds are not obvious to others instead concealed by feelings of worthlessness, self-loathing, and self-doubt that you may experience. Emotional Abuse is demonstrated through a person's words, deeds, and consistency of these behaviors. Abuse doesn't stop, even if it starts out slowly. When someone consistently uses hurtful words and engages in bullying behaviors that undermine their self-esteem and compromise their mental health, the relationship is typically deemed emotionally abusive. In order to maintain control over the other person, the primary goal of emotional abuse is to quiet, isolate, and damage them. One of the most difficult types of abuse to spot because it can be covert and subtle. It can, however, also be obvious and deceptive.

Emotional or Psychological abuse can undermine your self-esteem in either case, and you can start to question your views and reality. Finally, you might feel trapped. People who have experienced emotional abuse are frequently too hurt to remain in the relationship but also too terrified to walk away from it. As a result, the cycle continues until a solution is sought.

You may lose all sense of who you are if it is severe and persistent. Over time, the accusations, shaming, insults, criticisms, and gas lighting may destroy your sense of self to the point where you are unable to view yourself realistically. As a result, you could start to concur with the abuser and develop internal doubts. Once the abuser's goal is achieved, you are in captivity because you believe you are not worthy of love from others. When you eventually come to the conclusion that no one likes you, you can withdraw from friendships and isolate yourself. Friendships can be affected by emotional abuse because those who experience it frequently worry about how others perceive them and whether they really like them.

Anyone can be a victim of this abuse, regardless of their age or gender. It could be your spouse or love partner. It is also possible that the abusers are your business partners, family members or care taker. No one always acts perfectly in their relationships but when someone intentionally hurts you repeatedly, it becomes abusive. People's behavior that seeks to make you feel terrified or horrible about yourself is not acceptable. This type of abuse is more difficult to identify; yet, it is important to recognize it and get help as soon as possible considering it often acts as an introduction to physical abuse.

Abuse in emotional relationships can happen suddenly or slowly. Some abusers appear to be good partners at first and then begin to abuse once the relationship has been established. When this change in behavior occurs, you may feel astonished, perplexed and even humiliated. Contrarily, you are never at fault for violence, regardless of what the abuser may tell you or how your loved ones may feel about you for permitting the abuse. It can be difficult to determine if certain behaviors are emotionally or psychologically harmful particularly if you grew up seeing abuse. However, the behavior, like all other forms of domestic abuse, is intended to gain and maintain power and control over you.

Psychological abuse can be presented in different forms. Some of them are mentioned below. It involves someone consistently:

- Embarrassing you in public or in front of family, friends, support staff, or coworkers.
- Name calling such as "stupid", "disgusting", or "worthless"
- Threatening to hurt you, your family members, or people who are close to you.
- Treating you poorly because of things you cannot change; such as your religion, race, history, disability, gender, sexual orientation, or family.
- Ignoring you or acting as if you are not there.
- Doing and saying things that leave you baffled. This might involve someone moving or modifying something and then denying they did so.
- Always correcting what you say in order to make you appear or feel silly.
- Getting furious in a frightening manner.
- Threaten to harm themselves if they are angry with you.
- Acting overly obsessed and will not want you associating with others.
- Deciding for you what you should decide, such as what to wear or eat.
- Acting jealous, including accusing you of cheating on a regular basis.

If you consistently detect any of these attitudes, it indicates that you are abused. You do not deserve emotional abuse and it is not your fault if it occurs however, you should seek help immediately. Additionally, emotional abuse can result in a multitude of health issues. Abuse can lead to mental health problems such as depression, stress, and in rare cases, the formation of eating problems.

Physical effects of emotional abuse include developing stomach ulcers, irregular heartbeats, and sleeping disorders.

Chapter 2

Who can be an emotional Abuser?

Oftentimes when people hear the word "emotional abuse", their thoughts go to couples or people in some romantic relationship. It does not stop there. Emotional abusers are Individuals who mentally abuse others or allow it to happen to others. "Individuals" is emphasized. This implies that it might be anyone, irrespective of gender, age or relationship with the person in question. Abusers can be really attractive. He or she might initially come across as incredibly charming, thoughtful, kind, and engaging. They might use that charm to learn very private details about their victim, which would subsequently be exploited to their advantage. They frequently mistreat those who are close to them. Abusers often give the impression that their actions or words are only intended to hurt the victim.

There are various red flags that indicate emotional abuse. Remember that even if your partner, parent, coworker, or friend just does a few of these actions, your connection with these individuals is still emotionally abusive.

When thinking about your relationship, keep in mind that emotional abuse can often be covert. As a result, detecting the signs can be quite difficult. Take into account how you feel in your encounters if you're having trouble figuring out whether your relationship is abusive.

If you feel wounded, frustrated, puzzled, misunderstood, depressed, nervous, or worthless whenever you interact with the other person, your relationship is likely to be emotionally abusive. Also, avoid persuading yourself that "it is not that bad" and minimizing the other person's behavior. Nobody has the right to psychologically harm you.

Everyone, including you, deserves to be treated with compassion and respect.

Recognizing this can assist you in breaking the pattern of emotional abuse. Abuse of this kind can occur in any kind of relationship including:

- Lovers, boyfriends, girlfriends, partners, husbands, and wives are all examples of relationships.
- Ex-husbands, ex-wives, ex-boyfriends, ex-girlfriends, ex-partners, ex-husbands.
- Carers or paid support staff
- Parents, guardians, and other family members
- Adult-aged children
- Other people you live with or see on a regular basis, both inside and outside the home.

The target of the manipulation might not even be aware of it. Finding these patterns and making an effort to stop them are crucial. Regardless of the form it takes, emotional abuse can fall under one of several categories, depending on the abuser's intentions.

Are narcissists emotional Abusers?

Narcissistic Personality Disorder is a mental illness in which persons have an excessive sense of their own worth. They require and want too much attention and they want other people to admire them. People suffering from this disorder may be unable to understand or care about the emotions of others. They are not confident of their self-worth and are quickly upset by the slightest criticism beneath this mask of great confidence. A narcissistic personality disorder generates issues in many aspects of life, including relationships, job, school, and finances. When they do not receive the particular favors or acclaim they believe they deserve, they may be generally sad and disappointed.

People with this disorder may find their relationships difficult and unsatisfying, and others may dislike being around them. This disorder affects more men than women, and it usually develops in teenage or early adulthood. Some children may exhibit narcissistic features, although this is often expected for their age and does not imply that they will develop narcissistic personality disorder; narcissistic parents may place an excessive importance or admiration on their children, viewing them as superior to others.

Children may imitate a parent's narcissistic behavior such as self-inflated beliefs or arrogant behavior. This may result in the child developing narcissism. Due to the discomfort involved with these emotions, narcissists seek to redirect their feelings onto others. They may have grown up with narcissistic careers or witnessed abuse or terrible incidents that influenced their upbringing. This is not, however, an excuse for the emotional and/or physical violence they inflict on their victims.

Narcissistic abuse happens when a narcissist gradually manipulates and mistreats others in order to gain control over them, resulting in a toxic atmosphere filled with emotional, psychological, financial, sexual, or bodily harm.

Narcissists take advantage of those around them by gas lighting, sabotaging, love-bombing, lying, and twisting situations to their advantage. As a result, victims of abuse may suffer long-term consequences. There are numerous indicators of narcissistic abuse in every relationship, whether platonic, familial, or sexual. Narcissists use a variety of techniques to damage a person's reality and confidence in order to establish or maintain control over a relationship or marriage. They may make you feel insane, making you less likely to seek help from family and friends.

Because they are vindictive, self-centered, and dependent, narcissists are unable to feel empathy. It is imperative that you either end the relationship with the narcissist right away or learn how to set healthy boundaries in order to prevent further harm from being done to you. This is true regardless of the nature of the relationship you have with the narcissist, whether it be with a romantic partner, parent, friend, or your boss. There is nothing wrong with you if you are an empathy and discover that you are drawn to narcissists all the time. Unfortunately, the narcissist finds you appealing just by virtue of who you are. They get what they need from you and the supply you provide.

Having a narcissist in your life is physically, emotionally and psychologically taxing regardless of the circumstance you are currently in.

From all indications, narcissists are emotional abusers. Despite the fact that it is said to be a mental illness, it does not justify the fact that they mentally abuse their victims. Both the culprit and victim should seek help immediately.

Chapter 3

Can mental abuse escalate to physical abuse?

Domestic violence is commonly amongst couples. It is a pattern of actions done by one spouse in a relationship to seize and keep hold of authority and control over the other. To feel like they have control over their spouse, the abuser will do anything in their power. Things become more serious if they feel threatened. If one partner engages in any action to undermine the other's sense of self and mental wellbeing, the relationship is deemed emotionally abusive. When someone uses physical force to harm another, it is known as physical abuse. Physical Abuse is when someone uses physical force on you that could cause harm. If you experience emotional abuse, your relationship may eventually become physically abusive.

Violence against intimate partners does not always look the same or occur in the same way. However, there are some similarities that define it. No matter their age, ethnicity, country, socioeconomic background, culture, or level of education, it can happen to anyone. People who are subjected to mental abuse frequently end up being physically abused as well.

Most people who hurt their partners physically also hurt them emotionally or psychologically. A relationship will typically begin as loving and intimate. Abusive spouses take control through this promising beginning. Without that connection, someone would leave. But because of that connection, leaving becomes considerably more difficult. The abuse on an emotional and psychological level begins causing the partner to feel as though they are the victim of the abuse, alone, and unworthy. When physical abuse becomes regular, it first manifests as emotional abuse.

The word "escalate" means to increase in extent, volume, number, amount, intensity, or scope. Every abusive relationship has a tendency to worsen, but does mental or emotional abuse (using words to hurt the victim) progress to physical abuse (physically harming the victim)?

Even though each abusive relationship is unique, a cycle always exists. When you first meet your abusive partner, the cycle begins. They normally hook you before initiating the next phase of the cycle and never immediately reveal their abusive side. Abusers then proceed into the tension-building stage after the initial manipulation.

At this point, the abuser will start picking at the victim to raise tension.

The victim may be considered insecure by making offensive comments or engaging in other behaviors that raise tension. The victim frequently experiences anxiety or fear as a result of the change. At this point, communication in the relationship often deteriorates. This stage can persist for a single day or for several weeks. Things start to become serious at this point.

The following phase in the cycle is the abusive or "acting out" stage. Here is when the escalation really kicks in. This is typically where physical violence occurs. At this point, if the victim has only endured emotional abuse from their abuser, it may progress to physical abuse. During this phase, all types of abuse including those that are emotional, financial, sexual, and physical get worse. This shows that emotional abuse can start gradually via talks and threats and escalate suddenly to physical abuse. It is not true when an abuser claims they "lost control" or "did not mean it" when their abuse escalates. Abusers often decide to escalate when they feel they are losing control over the victim or when they want to make it absolutely obvious that they are the ones in charge of the situation.

When abuse intensifies, the abuser is essentially demonstrating that they have a new method of controlling the victim and overtime, the abuser's self-assurance grows. The next stage of their strategy to capture a survivor has begun. Escalation is not the result of anything the survivor did. A victim did not make an abuser "angrier" by doing or saying something; abusers decide whether to escalate or not to de-escalate their behavior. The victim should be aware of two things when the abuser has clearly escalated their abusive methods: The danger of leaving later will simply increase, and the situation may worsen.

Always keep in mind that verbal and emotional abuse might develop into physical violence at any time. Underestimating an abuser's power is the riskiest thing a survivor can do. It can be complicated when a victim of abuse keeps giving their abusive partner opportunities to change because they believe they love them.

Do They Change???

People change!

That two-word phrase actually makes a big, important point that has a lot of weight. We learn about change as we grow older, including its expected nature and potential for uncertainty.

Our beliefs, personalities, occupations, friendships, and other things change over time. But a common question is: Is it possible for an abuser to change?

Some changes appear to occur suddenly. Others require greater awareness because they must, such as kicking an addiction or changing a character fault that is damaging to oneself or others. It can seem hard to change a loved one when you are the one hoping for it, but we cling to the hope that they will do it because we remember how different they were in the past (and if they changed for the worse, can they not change for the better?)

You will never be able to change an emotionally abusive person by acting differently or by changing who you are, no matter how hard you try. A person who is abusive chooses to act in an abusive manner. Remind yourself that you have no influence over their behavior and that their decisions are not your fault.

It is entirely up to you how you respond to emotional abuse. Although it is possible for people to change, this is much easier said than done because it requires a strong desire to do so and a dedication to all parts of transformation without the influence of the victim.

When considering the reasons abusers abuse, it becomes evident that many of the underlying variables are learned attitudes and emotions of privilege and entitlement, which can be very challenging to actually change. As a result, only a very small number of abusers actually change their behavior. An abusive spouse could voluntarily enroll in a recognized batterer intervention program that emphasizes behavior, self-reflection and accountability as one aspect of changing.

Abusers' ability to change their behavior is a complicated and debatable issue. Even though most abusers are in severe need of rehabilitation, they either are not aware of it or do not want it. Some specialists think that if abusers are motivated to do so, they can change. Others think that once an abuser has acted abusively, it is uncertain that they will stop. According to research, it is rare for an abuser to agree to engage in the significant effort necessary for them to change their lives.

Even when a relationship appears to be ideal on paper, it may actually be quite abusive and toxic. You can still stop abusive behaviors towards your spouse, though it can be difficult to recognize when you are doing them. When you are in an abusive relationship, it can be difficult to recognize yourself or your partner as the abuser.

If you think you are the abusive spouse, it is critical to own up to your actions so that solutions can be found to stop the abuse. If you are not sure if you are abusive or not, stop and consider whether your partner appears afraid of you. Does your partner comply with your requests, even if they are not their favorites? Does your partner appear distant? Do you believe your partner withholds information from you? Let us assume that you indicated yes to the majority of these. It is likely that you are the one who is abusive in the partnership.

An abuser must first acknowledge that he or she is an abuser and is ready to turn a leave. That is the first step to change! Here are some signs that an abuser is willing to change.

- He or she admits to wrongdoing and is fully aware of past attitudes. There must be a realization of the kind of behavior that has been exhibited in past times which has led to a decision to change.
- He or she does not make excuses or blame others for their actions. An abuser that is willing to turn a leave will not blame the partner for displaying certain characters.
- Demonstrate respectful, kind and supportive behaviors. This is evidence to change. Displaying the opposite from what the victim is used to shows something different is happening. This can even put the victim in doubt because it is a new and different experience.
- They accept the consequences of their actions. For every action, there must be a reaction. Not every case of abuse ends well while for others it could be a

happy ending with a long process. Whatever the case may be, he or she should be willing to bear the consequences of their actions and be patient to the very end.

- They do not demand applause for making better steps to change. If an applause is required, maybe the change is not genuine.
- They exercise less control. For change to be recorded, the victim must experience total freedom on every level.
- They manage their emotions properly especially when angry. This is very much expected especially when the abuse has advanced to a physical approach. To prevent reverting to previous behaviors, an abuser who is open to change must possess emotional regulation and control skills.

These signs must be exhibited over time to be sure it is not pretense and the victim might find it hard to loosen up especially at the initial stage because it is a whole new experience. A crucial first step is realizing your harmful behaviors. Recognition is a powerful tool that can increase one's readiness to effect lasting change. With the right care, it is possible to teach someone to behave differently. Without it, aggressive behaviors could worsen, harming your spouse and creating enduring relationship problems.

Not all abusers change for the better and the victim should be ready to leave the relationship when it is due without feeling guilty or having regrets.

CHAPTER 4

Breaking Free!

Recognizing an emotionally abusive relationship is the first step in dealing with it. First and foremost, you must admit any instances of emotional abuse in your relationship that you are able to identify. You may regain control of your life by being open and honest about your experiences.

Invisible scars from psychological abuse cut deeply. It weakens your self-worth and gradually dampens your soul like an endless storm. As anxiety sets in, your confidence shrinks, and you start to doubt yourself, your mental health suffers. Your psyche is poisoned by those abusive remarks and the frequent criticism. You begin internalizing the negative and doubting all of your decisions. Your once-vibrant spirit also dims as a result of emotional abuse, which has suffocated it. Because abusers typically tighten their hold and put space between you and your support network, emotional abuse also keeps you alone. Then loneliness sets in, making you feel isolated and powerless to ask for the support and solace you so urgently need. The tarnishing of your reputation may be the most obvious consequence.

Abusers of your emotions attack your identity, shaping you into a hollow reflection of their desires. Your goals and aspirations fall by the wayside as a result of their dominance. Avoid rationalizing your own behavior by saying "it is not that bad" and downplaying the other person's actions. Everyone, including you, needs to be treated with respect and kindness. You can break the pattern of emotional abuse by realizing this.

Breaking free requires an understanding of how emotional abuse affects your mental health. It is time to recover your identity and treat the mental injuries you have sustained. Recognize your right to set limits and to specify what behavior is appropriate and inappropriate in your relationship. Make it completely obvious that you deserve to be treated with respect, decency, and love and that emotional abuse will not be accepted. Making your worth known is a potent manifestation of self-love. It demonstrates your awareness of your individuality as a person with goals, aspirations, and dreams. Keep your sense of self intact and do not let the emotional abuser undermine it. Celebrate your successes, play to your talents, and never accept anything less than what you deserve.

Setting boundaries and claiming your worth, though, will not be easy. Your resolve may be put to the test if the emotional abuser resists. Be persistent. Hold fast to your beliefs and do not let their manipulations make you swerve. Boundaries are not barriers that isolate you; rather, they are stepping stones to healthier connections.

Therefore, express your boundaries in an assertive and clear manner. Give your partner a firm grasp of your expectations and be ready to enforce them if they are not met. The strength and self-awareness needed to escape emotional abuse and begin a healing journey are crucial. In order to terminate an emotionally abusive relationship, careful planning and strategic application are needed. So to make a clean break, be patient and have a good exit plan in place. Being ready brings you one step closer to regaining control over your life as knowledge is power. Think about your safety. Make a safety plan that includes telling a trusted person about your situation in confidence, considering safe locations to go. Gather your resources and network of supporters first. Speak with reliable family members, friends, or institutions that specialize in assisting people in leaving abusive situations. They may offer priceless advice, support, and a secure foundation. Make sure you have financial freedom.

Gather crucial papers and anything else you might need later. Make plans to flee immediately if need be. Your safety is of utmost importance, and a well-considered plan might mean the difference. Here are some tips to breaking free:

- Consider yourself first when it comes to your physical and mental wellbeing. Give up attempting to please the abuser. Attend to your requirements. Make a decision that will encourage optimistic thinking and self-affirmation. In addition, make sure you get enough sleep and eat nutritious foods. You may deal with the daily challenges of emotional abuse with the help of these easy self-care techniques.

- Tell the abusive person clearly that you will no longer tolerate their yelling, name-calling, insulting, rudeness, etc. Afterward, explain what will occur if they decide to engage in this behavior. Tell them, for instance, that the conversation will end and you will leave the room if they insult you or call you names. The secret is to stick to your bounds. The other person will understand that their emotional abuse will not be permitted as a result of this.

- Experiencing emotional abuse in a relationship for any length of time may lead you to believe that you are seriously flawed. However, the issue is not with you. It takes the decision to abuse. Stop putting the blame on yourself for things that are out of your control.

- Avoid interacting with abusive people. In other words, do not try to justify yourself, appease the abuser's anger, demand something from them, or apologise for something you did not do if they try to argue with you, insult you, or frighten you. If you can, simply leave the situation. Engaging with an abuser only puts you at risk for additional violence and suffering. No matter how hard you try, you will never be able to appease their feelings. This will be useful if it has escalated to physical abuse
- Clearly express the end of your relationship and, if at all possible, cut all ties. Avoid contacting them by blocking their phone number and social media profiles.
- Counselors and therapists are helpful while escaping emotional abuse. They give you a private, secure setting where you may talk about your experiences, work through your emotions, and learn valuable things.

The tangled web of abuse will be untangled via therapy, revealing patterns and dynamics that may have kept you imprisoned. You learn coping mechanisms in therapy, develop resilience, and have a better sense of who you are and what you are worth. Professional aid is a brave move towards taking back your life rather than a show of weakness. These professionals have the skills, knowledge, and empathy to help you while you recover and develop.

Healing from the effects of emotional abuse and escaping its grip is a difficult but necessary process. To recover control of your life, it is essential to recognize the warning signs of emotional abuse in relationships and to prioritize your well-being. Keep in mind that God and your true self are where your hope, meaning, and purpose are found. You can discover healing and release from the bonds of emotional abuse by asking for help and fostering healthy relationships. Always keep in mind that you are deserving of respect, love, and consideration, and that you have the ability to restructure your life according to your own standards.

Chapter 5
Breathe Again!

After you leave an abusive relationship, healing takes time. Therefore, give yourself the room and time to heal. Use patience and self-compassion as you move through a spectrum of emotions. Feelings of rage, sadness, or confusion are acceptable. Knowing that each burn will bring you closer to being refined. Allow yourself to pass through that fire that will make you gold. Get back in touch with your true self. Find what interests you, hobbies, and dreams that may have been buried because of abuse. Spend time doing things that make you happy, fulfilled, and have a feeling of purpose to feed your spirit. Surround yourself with people who will help you to rise. Lean on your loved ones and community of supporters who can relate to and affirm your experiences. Their compassion, support, and love will be a balm. It might be challenging and even frightening to change your focus from "why" to "what". It is okay to ask "What should I do next?" also, "What makes me feel better?" It might be a process of trial and error and requires time to investigate. Everyone else's experience and healing will be unique to you, and they might even differ from your expectations. Keep this in mind, and more importantly, be patient and nice to yourself. Not only from the people in your life, but also from yourself, you deserve to be loved and respected.

Treating yourself properly is something you should do just because you deserve it. Whether it is taking long nature walks, indulging in a good book, or treating yourself to a relaxing bubble bath, seek refuge in pursuits that nourish your soul. You can refuel your energies and re-establish contact with your deepest ambitions by practicing self-care. Concentrate on developing a positive self-image; highlighting your qualities, recognizing your accomplishments and engaging in self-compassion. Surround yourself with positive affirmations to serve as a constant reminder of your worth and resiliency. These self-care guidelines will strengthen your health and raise your self-esteem from within. To hasten your healing process, think about getting treatment. A qualified expert may offer direction, resources, and tactics to aid in the healing process, self-esteem restoration, and setting up healthy boundaries in future relationships.

Exercise is a very effective healing technique. It can be a crucial step in developing resilience and reclaiming a sense of power and self-worth since it gives back survivors control over their bodies, lowers the effects of stress, and acts as a type of meditation. Exercise has been proven in studies to have a variety of positive effects on mental health, including lowering anxiety and depression, boosting mood and self-esteem, and assisting in the release of endorphins, which can help fight pain and depressive moods. Exercise also helps survivors clear their brains and concentrate on their current situation since it can act as a type of meditation. For people who have a hard time controlling their emotions, such as those who deal with anxiety, this can be especially helpful. Exercise can aid survivors in regaining a sense of body awareness, being present in the moment, and being rooted. To sum it, make an effort to cultivate healthy habits for your mental and physical health. Give a balanced diet, sound sleep and regular exercise first priority. The process of healing is irregular. There may be obstacles in your path, but every step you take is proof of your strength and courage.

No matter how tempting it may seem, do not jump into a relationship too soon. You are wrong if you are hoping that it will help you heal from the abusive one.

The euphoria of a new relationship might keep your mind off the trauma in the beginning.

However, until you get better and learn coping mechanisms, the trauma and ignored scars will keep coming back. Take time for yourself and figure out ways to reclaim your life. Your family and friends are definitely thinking about what is best for you. They might make an effort to set you up or constantly encourage you to start dating. However, it takes time to get the courage to move on from an emotionally abusive relationship and begin dating. Do not be forced into anything by anyone. If you are not ready, you should not feel obligated to be in a relationship. As you attempt to regain your self-assurance and faith in love, enlist their assistance.

Chapter 6

Love again with open eyes

Restarting a relationship after being in an abusive one can be extremely difficult. You may have lost faith in love after years of living in constant worry and anxiety in an abusive relationship. Following emotional abuse, you might not know how to maintain a healthy relationship. After experiencing such violence, you can continue to question your ability to find happiness and whether it is even possible to fall in love. It could be intimidating for you to start dating again after an abusive relationship. However, it is still possible to fall in love after experiencing emotional abuse and live a normal life. The healthy relationship you have always desired can be attained by having the appropriate support system, moving slowly, prioritizing self-care, and being open to love. You will regain your sanity as the mental confusion fades away.

The first and most crucial step in answering the question "how to have a healthy relationship after emotional abuse" is to forgive yourself for staying in the relationship longer than you should. This might make you feel humiliated, guilty, and resentful.

However, being sympathetic with yourself and figuring out what drew you to your abusive partner rather than condemning or criticizing yourself will help. You can better grasp the pattern you need to break with the aid of counseling. Discover what attracted you to your violent partner, and try to understand what kept you in that relationship for so long. You do not want to be duped by the same type of individual once more. When you are prepared to go back to dating haven endured emotional abuse, be honest with your potential partner about the abusive relationship you were in. The connection can be built on trust by being open and honest about each other's previous relationships.

Discuss how you were treated unfairly and what you are now seeking in a partner. Justify your trust concerns and how your abusive relationship harmed your sense of self. If your new partner will respect your boundaries and let you heal at your own time, then you can only move forward in the relationship. Never accept less than the best, and pay attention to any warning signs. When reactivated, flashbacks, recollections, or panic attacks are frequently experienced by abuse survivors.

They may repeat the traumatic experience and become protective in response to loud voices, shouting, arguments or any other sound, location that makes them think of the abuser. You might not be able to pinpoint every one of your triggers right away. Treat yourself well and allow yourself some space. Taking note of your triggers when they occur and discussing them with your spouse will help you manage them.

It is possible that you initially find it difficult to build lasting relationships and that you frequently wonder how to rebuild good relationships after emotional abuse. But keep trying to find love. If it comes out that your partner is abusive, learn to recognize your needs and this time, defend yourself. But do not look to your new spouse to make you whole. They can undoubtedly hasten your healing, but you still need to undertake the inner work. Because they are accustomed to it, victims frequently fall for someone who possesses identical personality features and behaviors.

Any relationship's primary cornerstone is trust. For victims of abuse, reestablishing trust is a challenging process. It appears logical that you find it difficult to lower your guard. You no longer believe in yourself or in other people.

However, you need to be willing to open up to chances once more if you want the fulfilling and healthy relationship that you so richly deserve.

It is not expected of you to believe everything that someone says. Start cautiously and gradually earn the trust of your new spouse.

Upon achieving your own personal liberation, it is time to draw the priceless lessons from your experience. By gaining knowledge and understanding from the past, you can avoid abusive dynamics in the future. Consider the trends and warning signs you noticed. Find any hints of disrespect, control, or manipulation that may have been present. Your armor will be this acquired knowledge, protecting you from similar pitfalls. Develop a solid sense of worth and set boundaries. Accept yourself as you are and do not accept anything less than the love, respect, and kindness you are entitled to. Keep your instincts in focus. When something feels strange, trust your gut and pay attention to your inner voice. Your intuition is a potent compass that points you in the direction of connections based on equality, mutual respect, and trust. Make a future free from abuse by using the lessons you learnt from your experience.

Conclusion

Now that you are aware of this, you may take action to release yourself from emotional abuse and begin living a life of fortitude, self-love, and limitless opportunity. You have the ability to free yourself and find the locks to the chains holding you back. Therefore, go with assurance and recognize that you have the ability to design a life free from emotional abuse. Although it will not be simple, the benefits are tremendous. As you heal, be kind and gentle with yourself. Remind yourself that it is okay to experience any emotions that arise, including confusion, fear, tension, and anger. There is no urgency to move over these emotions because they are a typical component of the healing process. You can experience them and sit with them because they are yours. It does not make you anything other than courageous to feel difficult emotions. Starting a new relationship after being in an abusive one could be challenging. Although the road to recovery may not be simple, it will undoubtedly be worthwhile. Remind yourself that it is possible to fall in love once more whenever you find yourself unsure of how to rebuild a good relationship following emotional abuse.

As long as you give yourself plenty of time to recover, forgive, and regain your self-confidence, you can be in a happy relationship. A greater sense of worth and belonging as well as less stress have been related to healthy relationships.